CUMBRIAN RAILWAY PHOTOGRAPHER

The William Nash Collection

by
Kate Robinson & Robert Forsythe

© Oakwood Press & Kate Robinson 2002

British Library Cataloguing in Publication Data
A Record for this book is available from the British Library
ISBN 0 85361 592 6

Typeset by Oakwood Graphics.
Repro by Ford Graphics, Ringwood, Hants.
Printed by Cambrian Printers, Aberystwyth, Ceredigion.

Dedication

In memory of William and Marjory Nash
with love and gratitude
Mary, Margaret and Kate.

Published by The Oakwood Press (Usk), P.O. Box 13, Usk, Mon., NP15 1YS.
E-mail: oakwood-press@dial.pipex.com
Website: www.oakwood-press.dial.pipex.com

Contents

Acknowledgements

Kate commissioned Robert Forsythe to research the historical aspects of this collection for the exhibitions and this volume. He has created a full catalogue of the material which is accessible through the internet at http://www.forsythe.demon.co.uk/nash.htm .

Kate wishes to thank Eden District Council's Penrith Museum, Eden Arts, Peter Van Zeller of the Ravenglass and Eskdale Railway, Tony Money archivist to Radley College, Alan Sutcliffe a one time colleague of William Nash's and other former employees of the LMS and BR, Jim Galley, Colin Dixon and others in the Hexham Photography Group, and her husband John and family members for their support which has enabled the first exhibition to be mounted as a retrospective memorial to her father's work in the 50th anniversary year of his death.

Our thanks to Messrs Sankey and Porter for allowing postcard reproductions to be made.

Further thanks are due to Michael Stone whose persistent encouragement over many years has ensured that this collection was not forgotten and to the Oakwood Press and its proprietors, the Kennedy family, for publishing this portfolio.

Foreword

When Kate Robinson first showed me prints from her late father's negatives, I was fascinated to look through the viewfinder of a young railway enthusiast, who had captured glimpses of the changing district in the 1920s. Small private companies like the local Furness Railway had just been amalgamated into a huge conglomerate, the London Midland & Scottish (LMS), which he was to join and rise within.

With precious film restricted by pocket money, when William Nash visited the little Eskdale Railway, he looked at places which I have long wanted to see and which no one else seemed to have photographed at the time. This schoolboy shot locomotives old and new going north, south, east and west at the onetime junction of Penrith, the lake steamers and many other sights, familiar yet always with an individual outlook.

What lay beyond these images was a lifelong interest in trains, a flourishing transport career and, with Grecian tragedy when the systems they had built failed in patchy fog, an untimely early death travelling with so many fellow railway officers in the horrific three train collision at Harrow & Wealdstone station 50 years ago.

Bill Nash had joined the LMS from school; a volunteer signalman during the General Strike, he was prevented by slight colour blindness from any future direct operational role. Nevertheless he soon made his mark in a particular niche in the rail industry, within the many dimensioned world of timetabling and train control.

No pointless paperchase here - planning, pathing and diagramming the locomotives, rolling stock and train crews was partly conceptual, partly very practical when steam traction demanded regular breaks for water, coal or fire cleaning. As day by day running was monitored and changed to suit traffic and resources, tasks that would now tax a powerful computer were solved by such gifted people. He understood that the railway was not just rolling stock and routes, but was a complex inter-related organism that served the public good.

Throughout World War II, the LMS made a significant contribution to the Home Front, and as assistant district controller at Rugby, Nash was in a key position at a crucial time. With Nationalisation of the railways, he stretched his wings, but soon returned to planning whence he was sorely missed. A particular honour among the many letters of condolence to his family was regret from the new Queen in regard to his services to the Royal Train.

It has been a very personal journey of discovery to print, locate and identify these scenes. Now through the signal efforts of Kate, her researcher, her publisher and her many supporters, not least in the museums and galleries of Cumbria for hosting a travelling exhibition, these snapshots of long gone summer days will endure and be enjoyed by a wider audience. Each a glimpse - not - gone for ever!

Peter Van Zeller
Ravenglass
July 2002

Introduction

William Nash was born at St Bees in 1909. Whilst a teenager, he became a railway photographer, producing work of considerable quality and interest. Many of the engines photographed were soon to be re-liveried or withdrawn. Others were members of small and unusual classes. His interest led to a career with the London Midland & Scottish Railway which was tragically cut short by his death in the Harrow Railway Disaster of 8th October, 1952. His work had never been presented to the public prior to 2000.

Nash's railway photography ranges from Jersey to Kyle of Lochalsh. As a Cumbrian, he was naturally fascinated by the London and North Western Railway (LNWR), the Furness Railway (FR), the miniature Ravenglass and Eskdale Railway (R&ER) and the associated Lake steamers.

Railway Photography as a hobby was in existence in the late Victorian period. Working with glass plate cameras was challenging especially in capturing a moving object. The advent of roll cameras with film in a roll, but not yet the 35 mm format camera popular through the second half of the 20th century, made the hobby much more accessible to ordinary people after World War I, which was also an era of increasing travel. It was this technology that Nash used. Nash home-processed all his films, cutting his negatives into single images.

William Nash was about 14 when he took his first photos of the Ravenglass and Eskdale Railway. These are dated August 1923 in his album - some of the very few images he dated. Two other comparable photographers well known to railway enthusiasts are P. Ransome-Wallis, who took his first railway photograph in 1917, and H.C. Casserley whose first was in 1919. Another 'name', Bishop Eric Treacy started in 1932. Treacy photographed in the North, always less popular than the South through reasons associated with money and access. This northern background makes Nash's work all the more interesting.

Nash was unlikely to have had any railway photographer companions where he lived, but he was reading the monthly *Railway Magazine* and he had been introduced to railway postcard collecting, then a widespread hobby. Those twin strands, and long school holidays during which he visited friends and relations all over the country, seem to have been the background against which Nash started.

Nash and the famous poet W.H. Auden can be spoken of in one breath. In addition to his youth and remarkable ability with the camera, Nash's work has another merit. Chance saw him being brought up largely in the Lake District just after World War I. The poetry of W.H. Auden, who was only two years older than Nash, provides numerous instances of how the same landscapes and railways could inspire art (e.g. *Mountains*). Railways whose presence only a few generations before had been regarded as abhorrent by the Lake District artists of the day like Wordsworth.

Nash and Auden are comparable, they were young artists producing quality work. One acquired world renown, the other not so. Nash's career moved from railway photography to railway management. Before that happened he was well placed as an enthusiast to witness the effect of the 1923 Grouping of the railways in the North West into the London Midland and Scottish Railway. This means that many of Nash's subjects were still in their pre-Grouping liveries, were about to be scrapped, or in some cases were used on the West Coast Main Line only for a short period. In the case of the former Furness Railway engines, they came from small classes, were used only in this particular area of Britain, some of which had short lives, others of which were Victorian antiques and all about to be obliterated by new standard LMS designs.

Nash's work stands on its own as railway photographic art. His pictures are memorials to rare and beautiful objects. Victorian locomotive design had been an exquisite blend of the functional and the sublime form: sometimes beauty even seemed to take precedence over mechanical success.

Steam locomotive photography is essentially object based. It was undertaken by men who found these machines to have life, machines that were generally built, driven and fired by men. It was a product of its age. That is a statement of fact and not a social judgement. That the Nash collection has been uncovered is entirely due to the determination and photographic ability of one of Nash's daughters.

Kate Robinson is the youngest of William Nash's three daughters. She is an accomplished amateur photographer in her own right, a member of the Hexham Photography Group. She grew up with a small selection of her father's landscape photographs of the Lake District and Scotland decorating their home. This early exposure to photography led to her first darkroom attempts in her early teens. A considerable amount of monochrome darkroom work has been undertaken intermittently since then. Her favourite photographers include the monochrome giants Ansel Adams, Edward Weston and Cartier-Bresson.

Monochrome photography has always seemed to Kate to be a highly sensitive and interpretive medium, and one which eminently suits railway photography. The black and white printer, through fine tuning, can create a range of images from the same negative, thereby responding to the perceived mood of any occasion.

After many decades knowing that her father's material could interest, in 2000 she determined to explore the subject. All the prints used in this volume have been hand prepared from the original negatives by Kate in her darkroom. Although it would have been possible to print them using digital computer technology, the interpretation sought has been more effectively achieved in the darkroom. This traditional method is in keeping with Nash's own work. Kate has used Agfa Neutol Warm Tone developer and Ilford resin coated Warm Tone paper in order to maximise the range of black tones. The postcards and a few photos for which negatives could not be traced have been reproduced using modern computer technology.

Nash's originals were presented as 6 x 9 cms contact prints from the negatives mounted in typical albums of the period. He never owned an enlarger. Nash had captioned the material usually identifying location, engine number and, less often, train description. Dates were hardly ever given. Dating the material has relied on establishing when individual engines changed liveries or were built/withdrawn and then comparing material to establish what groups of images may have been taken at any one time. Establishing Nash's various addresses has been of assistance. Most of the photographs can be dated to within two or three years.

Chapter One

Ratty

Eight views start this chapter of Ravenglass station known to have been taken in August 1923 and August 1924. They are dated in the original albums and from their location in the albums, it is clear that Nash's railway photography first focused on the novel, yet local to St Bees, Ravenglass and Eskdale Railway (or 'Ratty'). This had once been a 3 ft gauge mineral railway but from 1915 - in the middle of World War I - it was converted to 15 in. gauge, to become a largely pleasure operation. This was carried out by Wenman Bassett-Lowke and his associates. He was a famous model manufacturer based in Northampton who from 1899 largely pioneered the British model railway hobby. Others followed but Bassett-Lowke was to dominate the quality end of the market into the 1950s. His company worked between Gauge 00 which is 4 mm to the foot scale and the miniature gauge of 15 in. It is difficult to be exact regarding the scale used for 15 in. gauge but *Little Giant*, a predecessor of *Sans Pareil* is quoted by Bassett-Lowke as being to 3 in. scale. The gauge was originally pioneered by Sir Arthur Heywood at his home, Duffield Bank, just north of Derby. He termed it 'minimum gauge' and saw it as a commercial proposition for estate and not primarily pleasure use. Sir Arthur died in 1916 and the availability of his equipment was seized upon by the revitalised Ravenglass and Eskdale Railway leading to an esoteric collection of rolling stock which Nash saw.

THE ESKDALE MINIATURE RAILWAY.

A commercial postcard produced by the Locomotive Publishing Co. showing the route of the 'Eskdale Miniature Railway'.

The engine in the first image is *Sans Pareil*. This Atlantic was a Bassett-Lowke product of 1913 which was too small for work at Ravenglass. She was worn out by the end of 1926.

Pacific engine *Colossus* in the early 1920s at Ravenglass. N.G.R stood for Narrow Gauge Railways, the Bassett-Lowke-owned operating company which had revitalised the line. *Colossus* was the first 15 in. gauge Pacific ever built and was originally delivered by Bassett-Lowke to the 15 in. gauge enthusiast Captain J.E.P. Howey for use on his Staughton Manor Railway in Huntingdonshire.

The remaining views show that Ravenglass station was in a state of flux in this period. Note the new ballast work. The overall roof went back to 3 ft gauge days. It went when the station was entirely remodelled for the 1928 season. Early 15 in. gauge passenger stock was varied. The Bassett-Lowke-supplied original four-wheeled open coaches can be seen. The first picture shows two covered bogie coaches in the station. The one on the right was one of Sir Arthur Heywood's coaches (others are around the turntable). The carriage to its left came from another estate light railway. This was the 'glass coach' from Sir Robert Walker's Sand Hutton Railway near York. It was quickly worn out and became a summerhouse by 1928.

This picture with a heap of granite chippings fits well with the 1922 start of the granite traffic on the 15 in. gauge. The stone came from Beckfoot Quarry via a crushing plant at Murthwaite. This traffic was trans-shipped at Ravenglass and remained important for several decades.

Ravenglass station from the turntable end with the original 3 ft gauge station roof. This angle looks up the line. To the left are standard gauge wagons for the stone traffic. They stand on a siding that leads to the newly-erected tippler.

The next picture is taken by standing on the tippler. The standard gauge siding is very obvious to the right as is the Furness Railway signal box in the distance. This still exists but nowadays it controls some of the R&ER trackage.

Muriel outside Ravenglass engine shed on the Ravenglass and Eskdale Railway. This picture is another taken by Nash in 1923 and must be amongst his first images.

Another picture taken at Ravenglass on the same day (look at the clutter on the boiler top) shows *Muriel* as an eight-wheeled tank engine. She was not built as a 'miniature' engine. Her builder in 1894 was Sir Arthur Heywood. She worked his Duffield Bank Railway until 1916. After the 1926 season, large parts of the 0-8-0 *Muriel* were turned into the 2-8-0 *River Irt* which still works the line and which Nash pictured.

Nash photographed his mother (*right*) outside the former miners' cottages at Dalegarth in 1924. The engine is *Sir Aubrey Brocklebank* which was withdrawn in 1927. This location was once a junction in 3 ft gauge times for the line to the original passenger terminus of Boot and a mineral branch. When the 15 in. gauge reached Boot in 1917 problems appeared owing to the steepness of the last stretch. Between then and 1926 when the present Dalegarth station opened on the old mineral branch, the terminus moved around, first to Beckfoot and then in 1922 to this spot by the miners' cottages at Dalegarth. *Sir Aubrey Brocklebank* reminds us that this shipping magnate closely associated with Cunard was a key benefactor to the line between 1917 and his death in 1929. His home was near the railway at Irton Hall.

A scene at the intermediate station of Irton Road around 1924. Heywood coaches are already dumped to the left. Since 1930, there has been a loop here but from the advent of the 15 in. gauge in 1916 to 1930 there was only a group of three sidings seen to the left. The building in the distance functioned as a 15 in. gauge locomotive shed. The station handled a considerable amount of freight into the 1930s. Timber, potatoes, the mail, sheep's fleeces all featured and one tale of the latter was converted into a story in Reverend Awdry's book *Small Railway Engines*.

A view of the crushing plant installed by Henry Greenly at Murthwaite by the Ravenglass and Eskdale Railway for the traffic from the Beckfoot Quarry in 1922. Crushed granite was only carried on the 15 in. gauge until 1929 when standard gauge tracks were laid as far as the plant.

Stone was brought in wagons from the quarry face further up the line at Beckfoot to the crusher at Murthwaite as in this picture. The wagons arrived on top of the crusher and tipped their load, which was crushed. Finished product left from the low level.

Handling the stone at Ravenglass on the tipping dock which was used between 1922-29. The engine is *River Irt*, ex-*Muriel*, which puts the picture between 1927-29. Its appearance at Ravenglass with four-wheeled stone wagons is a very rare picture, perhaps unique. There were internal combustion locomotives for this traffic. These wagons were usually used between Beckfoot Quarry and Murthwaite Crusher.

The dock looks very new in this picture, which is likely to be from 1924.

5376   NARROW GAUGE RAILWAY, ESKDALE VALLEY.

Nash collected railway postcards, before starting railway photography. The next five reproductions from Nash's cards take a journey up Eskdale. The first three are 'Sankey' cards. In original N.G.R. livery *Sans Pareil* has a small train of four-wheelers beside the Mite marshes near Ravenglass. The coaches were built by Bassett-Lowke like the engine, a number coming with it from an exhibition at Oslo to re-equip the line. These were the first 15 in. gauge rolling stock. The old 3 ft gauge sleepers are obvious.

8428 NARROW GAUGE RAILWAY, ESKDALE VALLEY.

The two scale model Pacifics working overtime.

6941   NARROW GAUGE RAILWAY, ESKDALE.   SANKEY, BARROW.

Heavily laden four-wheelers at harvest time approach Irton Road. The scale semaphore bracket signal controlled the main line for which the train is signalled and admission into the siding shown in Nash's picture previously *(page 17)*.

IRTON ROAD, ESKDALE

Irton Road station. The 3 ft gauge era station building remains in use today. The card was produced by J.D. Porter of Eskdale Post Office, whose descendants we thank.

Colossus (wrongly spelt) with a train including Heywood bogie open coaches is not at Boot but is really beside the erstwhile miners' cottages at Dalegarth in the 1922-1925 period. The card is from the Abrahams series.

Chapter Two

Standard Gauge in Cumbria

In looking at Nash's pictures of standard gauge steam in Cumbria, there is good reason to start at Penrith. He was evidently taking pictures there within a year or so of taking up photography. Judging by the number of images from Penrith, it was his most popular location after the Ravenglass and Eskdale.

From St Bees it would have been his nearest location on the West Coast Main Line of the LNWR/LMS railway. The chance to see crack expresses and the famous LNWR engines that hauled them was a must to the young Nash. A number of Nash's images appear to have been influenced by his work on the LMS in Southern Lakeland. North Cumbria is therefore largely ignored, there are no images in the collection of Carlisle and points between to Workington. Nash evidently did pass through these places as the collection does have some appealing material on branchlines in Dumfries and Galloway.

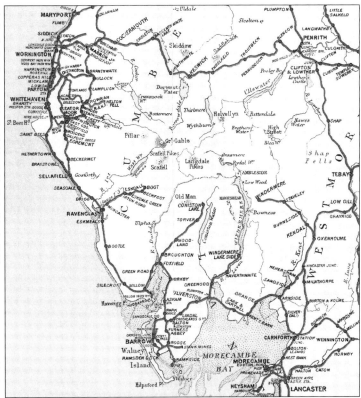

Railway Clearing House map showing the post-Grouping railways and the most prominent geographical features in the Lake District.

27

Where electrics now hum, but otherwise recognisable, No. 1678 *Airey* is in LNWR livery working southbound at Penrith. One of Webb's 'Precedent' class, the 6 ft 9 in. driving wheels helped create a Victorian thoroughbred. Built in 1892, withdrawn in February 1927, she was still in her LNWR livery when Nash photographed this engine in her Indian summer on the main line. *Hardwicke* is the sole survivor of this class.

A Webb 'Cauliflower' at Penrith. Once there were 310 of these machines current between 1880-1955. They were a standard LNWR goods engine but capable of taking the branch train from Penrith to Keswick as this one was about to do. The LNWR 87 numberplate is prominent. 'How . . . I wish I stood now on a platform at Penrith, Zurich or any junction at which you leave the express for a local that swerves off soon into a cutting . . .' W.H. Auden *Mountains*.

Whilst the 'Cauliflower' went west, a North Eastern Railway engine prepares to head east from Penrith, over Stainmore, to Darlington. This North Eastern Railway line existed between 1862-1962 and along with the Cockermouth Keswick and Penrith Railway was a key link between industrial Teesside and West Cumbria. No. 1464 is a Victorian product of 1885. Twenty of these express engines had been designed by Tennant. In the 1920s they were put out to grass on the Stainmore route prior to all being withdrawn by 1929. The engine is still in its full pre-Grouping livery, the green used by the North Eastern contrasting with the funeral black of the LNWR. The class leader No. 1463, withdrawn in 1927, was preserved. Today it can be found in Darlington North Road Station Museum.

This might be a monochrome picture but LMS No. 5950 is sparkling in its first coat of newly-applied LMS crimson lake. No. 5950 had been LNWR 116, a 'Claughton' class express engine built in 1917. The cab sides carry small letters 'LMS' which was the first insignia the company adopted in 1923. This livery was applied to the engine in November 1923. In the background are antique (even then) coal wagons and Penrith's red sandstone castle.

Nash was able to photograph the same engine or class repeatedly. This is a second interpretation of No. 5950 at Penrith. On this occasion the train is a Glasgow/Edinburgh to Liverpool/Manchester train. Most of the coaches retain LNWR colours.

Another Glasgow/Edinburgh to Liverpool/Manchester express heads south from Penrith. The engines faced 13 miles of climbing to Shap Summit largely at 1 in 125, the railway version of a 1 in 12 road gradient. Hence the use on this train of a pilot engine. This retains its LNWR number and name plates being their No. 124 *Marquis Duoro*. Behind it is LMS No. 10474 built in February 1925 which only lasted 10 years. No. 124 lost this number in May 1928 which sets the datelines for many of Nash's Penrith pictures.

This time LMS No. 10474 is working solo whilst heading north at Penrith. These engines were known as the Hughes 'Dreadnoughts' and had first been built for the LNWR's associate, the Lancashire and Yorkshire Railway, in 1908. More were built to a slightly different design at the time of the railway Grouping. Their association with the Lancaster and Carlisle line was not very happy although the final 20 built, of which this was the last engine, worked from Carlisle Upperby depot.

Nash found the classmates to No. 10474 interesting. A workstained LMS No. 10464 heads north through Penrith. Accepting these pictures cannot be any earlier than 1924 and are likely to be mid-1920s, the survival in both this and the previous print of the two-tone dark chocolate and white colours of the former LNWR coaches is noteworthy.

A wet day at Penrith. *Miranda* prepares to pilot *Prince Albert* south. Engines and coaches are all in LNWR livery. Milk churns remind us that the railways were once vital to the dairy industry. The front engine had a 33 year working life until 1930, the second engine only lasted 15 years to 1934. The latter's name was applied in February 1922 and its LNWR livery was removed in February 1926. The train is an Aberdeen-London service.

Suvla Bay at Penrith in a scene that is almost entirely pure LNWR. *Prince Albert* and *Suvla Bay* were both members of the LNWR's 'Prince of Wales' class introduced in 1911. The LNWR's naming policy was wide-ranging but strongly influenced by railway imperialism or patriotism. A number of World War I-built engines had related names. Suvla Bay featured in the disastrous Gallipoli campaigns of 1915.

The straight line across the region was the Lancaster and Carlisle line of the LNWR. The ascent of Shap, south of Penrith, usually appealed to photographers but Nash only took two photographs around Shap. The 2 pm goods from Carlisle storms through Shap station. One of the LMS's few really successful early designs was the so-called Horwich 'Crab' - built at Horwich works. LMS No. 13029 was built in 1927, changed number in the mid-1930s and lasted until 1963. Shap station closed in 1968.

North of Shap, the 1.35 pm goods from Carlisle works up the 1 in 125 gradient through limestone country at Thrimby Grange. Engine No. 9641 was built for the LMS in 1932, part of a 175-strong class known as 'Austin Sevens'. Despite their bulk, they were not a great success. The evidence suggests these two pictures date around 1933-35.

The subject of this Nash picture taken at Lancaster looks like a West Coast express in difficulties. No. 10449 was a classmate of engines which Nash photographed at Penrith. In origin the design came from the Lancashire and Yorkshire Railway and these engines were never enthusiastically adopted on the run through Cumbria. Judging by the ex-LNWR tank engine on the front and the crew by the cylinders something was amiss. This was also the southern terminus for Furness trains from the coast.

At Carnforth the Furness trains gained their own tracks and headed for the coast from what had become a major railway junction for three companies. The massive bulk of this engine under Carnforth's overall roof belongs to Furness Railway No. 118, the last but one engine delivered to the company. It is working a Whitehaven to Lancaster train.

The reason for No. 118's bulk is evident in another picture taken at Carnforth. It is a so-called Baltic tank with a 4-6-4T wheel arrangement. The engine was delivered late in 1920 but these five engines were scrapped between 1934-40 as non-standard on the LMS.

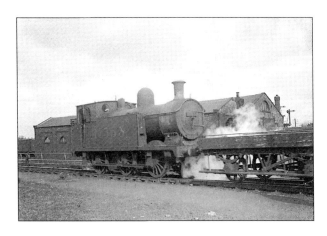

Three of Nash's images of engines at the Furness locomotive shed at Carnforth follow. The first shows LMS 0-6-0T No. 11553, a former Furness Railway engine. It belonged to a modern class of eight engines built between 1910 and 1916. None achieved a long life being withdrawn between 1930 and 1943. They were quite powerful shunting engines, this one had been first Furness No. 19 and then 55 and it was the class leader.

Tucked away in a siding at Carnforth was LMS No. 10138, ex-Furness No. 45, 4-4-0. Nash found the Furness 4-4-0s appealing and since they were not long for this world that is fortunate. No. 10138 was one of a class of eight, all of which had gone by 1931 having been built between 1896-1900. Their maker was Sharp, Stewart.

Another of the Furness 4-4-0s was LMS No. 10145, ex-FR No. 128. This example came from a class of four built in 1900-01 which were withdrawn after 30 years' service. Their 6 ft 6 in. diameter driving wheels intended them for fast passenger work. Here it is drifting off Carnforth shed since Nash's next negative (reproduced two pictures forward) portrayed it on a train. The previous two pictures are numbered in such a manner by Nash as to suggest they are considerably earlier than this picture which is likely to be taken between 1929-31.

'Furness and Midland Junction' is Nash's caption which places this and the next prints just outside Carnforth station which was to the right of the picture. Nash took a sequence of pictures here, apparently on a bleak winter's day of low light and condensing steam. The double-headed train was the 10.45 am Carnforth to Grange-over-Sands. Behind the Furness 0-6-0 tender engine (LMS No. 12475, once Furness No. 14) was a new LMS 2-6-4T tank engine No. 2359. This engine, designed by Fowler, means that these pictures must have been taken in 1929 or later.

It was not much warmer when the 12.10 pm from Carnforth to Whitehaven left. The engine is LMS No. 10145, once Furness No. 128, again. This sequence of Furness and Midland photos can therefore be dated to between 1929 (when the Fowler 2-6-4T was built) and 1931 (when No. 10145's class was extinct).

Facing the other way (the west), at Carnforth Furness and Midland Junction, Nash photographed No. 2359 returning from Grange on the 11.25 am to Carnforth. He had evidently engaged in an hour or so's linesiding on a cold winter's day.

LMS No. 8796, one of the LNWR Whale-designed 19 in. goods engines has come completely off the rails just outside Carnforth station. These scenes are notable for the presence of a breakdown train. 'Loco Dept Tool Van' can be made out on the 'birdcage'-roofed van to the left of the engine.

The men in bowler hats and flat caps are in evidence. The bowler hat was perhaps the district traffic officer. Re-railing is not being done with a crane but with manually operated jacks and timber packing.

Viewed head on, it is clear how completely derailed No. 8796 was. One of Carnforth's LNWR signal boxes surveys the scene. Nash by now was employed by the railway at Carnforth which probably explains how he got access to take these pictures. He was living at nearby Arnside between December 1928 and 1932.

The Furness route had to cross several estuaries like the Kent at Arnside. LMS No. 12947 had been Furness No. 26, one of their more powerful 0-6-0 goods engines built during the company's last decade. It has a long train of empty coke wagons returning from Barrow steelworks to Tebay, and thence the Stainmore line to the cokeworks of County Durham. A cut-off line ran from Arnside to Hincaster for these trains, for which the train is signalled.

LMS No. 10186 had been Furness Railway No. 131, one of four engines built in 1913/14 and withdrawn in 1932/33. This small class was the last Furness 4-4-0 design. These Arnside images with the trains in full LMS colours probably date from about 1929 and Nash's time working for the railway at Carnforth.

A further Arnside image shows LMS No. 11103, one of the former Furness Baltic tanks hauling the 9.53 am Carnforth to Whitehaven service.

There were two Furness branches to the Lakes. One to Lakeside on Windermere was for its final 20 years under British Railways only operated seasonally. A part now survives as the Lakeside and Haverthwaite Railway. This LMS-era train on the Lakeside branch is at Newby Bridge. The engine on this former Furness branch was one time Midland Railway No. 3730, a '3F' 0-6-0 freight engine that is almost certainly hauling an excursion train from Leeds or Bradford. Nash noted the train as coming from the 'Midland Section'.

Nash's other photograph on the Lakeside branch shows the branch goods at Newby Bridge. Three wagons and a brake van from Lakeside to Ulverston are being hauled by LMS No. 11630, which was once Furness 103. This was one of the 10 Furness Railway class 'L2' 0-6-2T built in 1904. A slightly different Furness 0-6-2T was caught at Whitehaven and appears further on in the chapter. Both these Newby Bridge images have been reproduced by scanning from the contact print as the original negatives appear to have been lost. Their quality is not the best but their subject interest is considerable.

The second branch reached Coniston from Foxfield. This line originally had ore traffic as much in mind as lake passengers. When it opened in 1859, the railway-owned *Gondola* (seen in the next chapter) took up service on the lake, whilst the line went for another half a mile beyond the station to a trans-shipment point for copper ore from Coniston mines. Nash captured LMS No. 11084 arriving at Coniston. This had been Furness No. 42. Interesting details are the ground signal in the foreground and the Furness-liveried Loco Coal wagon.

Sparkling in the sun LMS No. 11084 runs round the branch train at Coniston. Kitson in Leeds built this engine in 1916 for the Furness Railway. The class of six had gone by 1933, a premature end for such handsome machines. The lining out of the livery can be detected and the LMS emblem on the bunker pushes the picture into the mid-1920s or a little beyond. It is likely that the locomotive was gleaming in crimson lake, this combination of emblem, colours and numeral typeface became redundant in 1928. In the second picture another Loco Coal wagon can be glimpsed. It was probably coupled to the Furness example in the last picture but this one had gained LMS livery. Coniston became one of the first LMS stations to host camping coaches. This was in 1934 and sadly, by then, Nash had left the area.

As the Furness line turned north beyond Millom it skirted the lower slopes of Black Combe making for this image. Nash's original was uncaptioned. Mapwork (hopefully) gives the location. The engine is the Stanier 1935 2-6-4T design for the LMS which makes the picture a 'late Nash', a point confirmed by the steel-sided vans at the front of the train and only one former Furness (low-roofed) coach.

Where the Furness lines crossed the Esk and the Mite at Ravenglass there was a junction with the Ravenglass and Eskdale Railway. The buildings are still recognisable but the trains are not. Nash photographed former Furness Railway engines at Ravenglass in both the old Furness livery and the new LMS crimson lake. The engine is one of the Furness Baltic tanks that appealed to Nash and which have been seen previously. Other pictures of these engines were taken at Ravenglass. This one in full Furness livery is No. 118 on a Barrow-bound train.

On a different occasion Nash photographed former Furness Railway No. 133, now repainted into LMS colours and re-numbered 10188 on the tender. There were only four of these which worked for about 20 years from 1913. In their heyday they handled Barrow-London trains as far as Lancaster. A sister has been shown earlier. The stock seems still to be in the Furness colours of blue and white.

The northern extremity of the Furness Railway's coastal route was Whitehaven Bransty station. Caught there in its Furness livery was their 0-6-2T No. 111. This had been built in 1907 as a member of the six-strong 'L3' class. Sawn timber seems the predominant load for the train.

Working tender first out of the tunnel into Bransty station is Furness Railway 0-6-0 No. 6. It is hauling a local passenger train from the Cleator line. There were 16 engines in this class which existed between 1899-1936.

No. 6 (but officially by now LMS No. 12483) runs round its train at Bransty. The Furness Railway numerals 'No. 6' are clear on the bufferbeam. There was an island platform behind the engine where the coaches had been left. To the right of the engine is the town gasworks and beyond that the William Pit. That colliery was the scene of a terrible disaster in 1947 in which 104 miners lost their lives.

This venerable Furness antique emerging from the tunnel at Bransty had gained LMS numbers on its tender as its No. 12007. There had been 55 of these engines built from 1866 and all gone by 1927. They were nicknamed 'Sharpies' after their builders Sharp, Stewart and Co. The four-wheeled tender with its external springs and a chimney towering over the locomotive all suggest age. This engine had been Furness No. 62.

There were numerous Cumbrian railway byways away from the West Coast Main Line or the Furness system. One was the ex-North Eastern Railway's branch running along the South Tyne Valley to Alston. London and North Eastern Railway No. 1640 sits outside Alston's small loco depot. This was one of 20 long-lived engines current between 1893 and 1955. This scene is a car park today but since closure in 1976, the narrow gauge South Tynedale Railway has successfully reinstated the southern end of the line.

Chapter Three

Afloat in Cumbria

Long-standing lake services have been operated on four of the Cumbrian lakes. These are Windermere, Ullswater, Coniston and Derwentwater, in rough order of importance and extent. Services continue today but with no railway ownership. The privatisation of Sealink in 1984 closed that chapter. Windermere and Coniston had seen railway services. On Windermere there were considerable elements of competition at different times, whilst on Coniston many decades passed with no service at all from World War II. The award for long-lived continual service with one operator goes to the Ullswater Navigation and Transit Company and its two vessels.

Since the railway did not offer through routes within the Lake District, apart from the Penrith-Keswick line, a complicated network of combined tours became well established over the years using a combination of road, water and rail travel.

Although Nash was working at Windermere early in his railway career, no pictures were found of that branch from Oxenholme to Windermere. He may have felt it inappropriate to use the camera as a junior member of staff in a new job. Windermere station is a long way from the lake and had been part of the LNWR system, whereas the steamers and their connecting branch at Lakeside were Furness owned.

Above right: A view from Nash's mother's album taken on Ullswater in 1925. William Nash can been seen in the centre of the boat.

Left: SY *Swift* leaving Bowness Bay. This 1900-built steamer (Seath of Rutherglen) survived into the 1990s, latterly from 1957 as a diesel vessel. She was then broken up. This is an Abrahams of Keswick card.

The Ullswater steamer *Lady of the Lake* at anchor. Ullswater is south-west of Penrith and has never had a rail connection. The steamers, which were motorised in the 1930s, have always been operated by the Ullswater Navigation and Transit Company since 1855. *Lady of the Lake* arrived in 1877.

The next three images show Glenridding pier hosting the Ullswater steamer *Raven*. *Raven* looks quite different today with a very prominent upper deck wheelhouse forward.

Both *Lady of the Lake* and the 1889 *Raven* continue to operate. Vessels that Nash photographed have stayed at work on their homeground long after the contemporary steam engines have disappeared. The long trails of smoke or steam on Nash's pictures indicate that he used quite slow shutter settings.

Helvellyn seen from St Sunday Crag (accessed from Glenridding Pier). The steamers have always been a way for the visitor to reach favoured walks and Nash followed the pattern.

Ullswater from near today's Aira Force car park.

Real excitement: Nash portrays the Windermere cargo steamer *Raven* at work at Ambleside. Another of his photographs shows her at Lakeside. Unlike the Ullswater *Raven*, the Windermere example was built in 1871 for the Furness Railway as the lake's freight boat. Here she is in LMS hands, though in 1927 she was sold to Vickers Ltd. Later she sank before being rescued for the Windermere Steamboat Museum.

Tern is well laden at Ambleside. This 1891 steamer is now the oldest at work for the main Windermere fleet. Built for the Furness Railway by the Forrest shipyard near Colchester, like certain other Lake steamers, she was of a pre-fabricated type commonly used around the British empire.

Nash noted this as the LMS steam yacht *Swan* off Ambleside. The *Swan* in use today was built for the LMS in 1936 to replace the vessel Nash photographed. The first *Swan* had been built in 1869 for the Windermere United Steamboat Company. She sank twice in her career.

S.Y. "CYGNET" OFF LAKE SIDE (WINDERMERE)

Nash's postcard collection included the Lakeland steamers as well as railway trains. These next three cards are of the Windermere fleet. They are part of a set entitled 'English Lake Steamers' produced by Tuck for the Furness Railway. *Cygnet* was in service on Windermere from 1879-1955.

S.Y. "CYGNET" & "TEAL" OFF AMBLESIDE

COPYRIGHT

Cygnet and *Teal* were 1879 sister ships. Neither now exist, *Teal* became redundant as early as 1927.

S.Y. "BRITANNIA" FOR HIRE BY PRIVATE PARTIES ON WINDERMERE

'SY *Britannia* for Hire' is the significant title of this Furness Railway postcard for a vessel that only worked in its fleet for seven or eight years. She had been a private steam yacht of 1879 that the Furness bought in 1907. Some of her fixtures are reputed to exist still in local homes.

One of Nash's gems is his view of both of the railway steamers based at Coniston. The *Gondola* is in the foreground. Owing to her restoration by the National Trust, this extravagant 1859 vessel is well known. Behind her is the far more modern 1908 *Lady of the Lake*. This came from the Thornycroft yard in Southampton. Although this vessel passed to British Railways (unlike *Gondola* which had been sold for use as a houseboat), she never worked after World War II and was dismantled in 1950.

S.Y. "LADY OF THE LAKE" ON CONISTON LAKE

COPYRIGHT

Lady of the Lake had a namesake on Ullswater, the name being derived from the Arthurian legend. The Furness Railway issued more than 160 cards, and a large number featured their vessels which also included services across Morecambe Bay from Barrow. The company's steamers were also featured on posters which were themselves reprinted as postcards.

Chapter Four

The Lure of the Fells

Nash was a Cumbrian by birth and by inclination, although he was sent south for his schooling, and his mother spent time at Cheltenham, whilst Nash grew up. We know that his first paid employment saw him back in the Lakes working for the LMS at Windermere and Carnforth. The fells were already well known to him from his boyhood and from Lakeland summer holidays earlier in the 1920s. The evidence from the negatives used is that Nash's landscape pictures were taken on his second camera. All these pictures were taken between 1924 and 1936.

Alston claims to be England's highest market town. Its heyday came with lead mines in the Georgian and early Victorian period, from which times its style remains. In 2001 it capitalised on this with the filming of 'Oliver Twist'. This Dickensian atmosphere prompted Nash to use the camera. Apart from his cycle, what else is 20th century? It is quite likely that the image was taken on the same day as that at the bottom of the hill where Nash took his picture at Alston station which closed Chapter Two. Alston was in Cumberland but it was still a very long distance for Nash to travel. Perhaps he took the train one way and then cycled across the Hartside road - down or up? Nash was never a car owner and nor would his wife ever be.

Much nearer his regular stamping ground, Nash photographed Stanley Ghyll or Force or Dalegarth Force. This waterfall enjoys a variety of names. It is up a ravine on the south side of the Esk about a mile from either the present Dalegarth station or from the Beckfoot Halt adjacent to which is the building of the Stanley Ghyll Hotel dating from the 1890s. Alfred Wainwright wrote 'This is deservedly the most popular walk from Dalegarth Station'.

A valley or so north of Ratty, Nash found Wastwater. This is England's deepest lake and often regarded as one of the most sombre of the Cumbrian lakes. It remains quite unexploited with no steamer service and the famous scree slopes which tumble down to the south-eastern shore. The portrait looks to the north-east end from which there are well known routes to Scafell Pike and Sca Fell. Yewbarrow is the prominent summit to the left, thence Great Gable and Lingmell.

One of the most favoured of accesses to the high summits takes the visitor past Elterwater and Chapel Stile to the head of Great Langdale. Nash made the trip and took this picture looking up Langdale just beyond Chapel Stile.

One reward for his efforts was this view of the Langdale Pikes taken from across the valley on a path ascending The Band up to Bow Fell. The late Neolithic stone axe factory is on the slopes of the picture's left side around the area of lighter scree.

With snow highlighting their features Nash pictured Sca Fell (3,162 ft) and Scafell Pike (3,210 ft) from around the summit ridge of Bow Fell. These are England's highest mountains. Railway enthusiasts will recognise *Scafell Pike* as the name of British Railways No. D1, the first of the express 'Peak' class diesels, in use between 1959 and 1976. Nash never photographed any diesel traction.

A circular walk up The Band, along Bow Fell, along to Esk Hause, back to Rosset Pike and thence down Rossett Gill or along the ridge of the Langdale Pikes is possible as a walk from Langdale. It is a walk familiar to Nash's youngest daughter. Nash labelled this scene as Great Gable from Esk Hause. Hause is the Lakeland term for a crossing point through a ridge. *Great Gable* was another 'Peak' class diesel, No. D4. Bow Fell was never a member of that class but many years later a class '60' diesel, No. 60015 was named *Bow Fell* and featured in the launch of the short-lived Transrail freight company at Warrington on the 5th September, 1994. Other class '60s' carried names relevant to these pictures these were, Nos. 60006 *Great Gable*, 60016 *Langdale Pikes*, 60049 *Scafell* and 60097 *Pillar*. All except *Bow Fell* had lost these names by 2000.

Borrowdale from Cat Bells, a peak that is one of Lakeland's easiest and loveliest. It allows the valleys of Newlands and Borrowdale to be superbly appreciated. In the middle of the picture the houses of Grange can be made out. The peak seemingly rising from the valley floor is Castle Crag and in the flat valley bottom beyond that is Rosthwaite.

No railway ever penetrated Borrowdale although Derwent Water hosts a boat service (the only one of the four major Lake services not portrayed by Nash). The road up Borrowdale climbs out via the Honister Pass. Nash used this road and took this image of the western side of the Honister. Nash certainly enjoyed minor railways and it did not escape him that at Honister his picture could include a slate quarry and its transport systems. The stone exploited is the famous Westmorland Green Slate. Nash is standing high above the road (just visible extreme bottom left). Immediately below his vantage point the tracks of the tramway from the Honister Hause slate mill to the Yew Crag workings run. Prominent on the opposite side below the summit of Fleetwith Pike is the well-engineered route to the workings at Bull Gill. This man-made ledge was called The Monkey Shelf and took carts to tramways in Bull Gill itself.

After all the effort of the Honister which is through the central valley of this image, the delights of Buttermere were relaxing. There is a low level and well maintained shore path, or, as Nash appeared to have taken, there is a higher route above Burtness Wood. The big house, whose roof is catching the light to the left, is Hassness.

Nash could record sylvan low level Lake District scenes. This one is thought to be between Crummock Water and Buttermere looking to the latter.

Nash was standing on the ridge of Red Pike for this picture. Ahead and to the left the ridge climbs to High Stile. The drop on the left is down to Bleaberry Tarn and and thence Buttermere some 2,000 ft below. The valley beyond is Ennerdale and on its far side the fell rises to Pillar at 2,927 ft.

The ascent of Red Pike that Nash had followed went past Bleaberry
Tarn creating this fine view.

A dramatic view closes this section. This is Ennerdale seen from the Red Pike whose summit occupies the watershed between Buttermere and Ennerdale. Ennerdale is one of the least frequented of the Lakeland valleys, its outlet leading to the west is the River Ehen which reaches the sea at Sellafield. In the foreground the River Liza feeds it from the slopes of Great Gable. This lonely valley was the nearest major Lake District valley to St Bees.

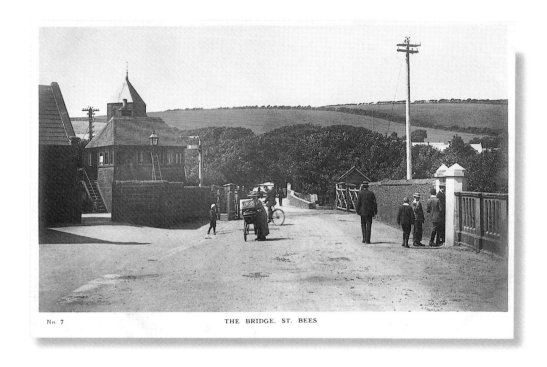

No. 7   THE BRIDGE. ST. BEES.

A period postcard in the Moss series of The Bridge, St Bees.   *Kate Robinson Collection*

Chapter Five

A Biographical Excursion

William Nash was born at St Bees in 1909. St Bees is at the most westerly point of the Cumbrian coast. Nash's collection includes a number of postcards of the place. In the view opposite, two key themes are evident: the railway signal box is still there in 2002, the line having first opened in 1849, the boater-adorned schoolchildren belong to St Bees School. This also continues to influence the community today but it is rather older than the railway, having been founded by Archbishop Grindal in 1583. Most of the buildings are Victorian or Edwardian and it was in this expansive atmosphere that Nash's parents came to St Bees. They were William and Ida and William was a schoolteacher with St Bees School (*see overleaf*).

Their union produced one child, the William of this book. Sadly William Nash the younger was only just over a year old when his father died prematurely. It would have been likely that Nash would have grown up around the school shown in this card. As things turned out, long holidays were spent at St Bees in the house that the Nashes had had built for them but William's mother had a pressing need to make a living which she did as a Matron in a preparatory school.

Consequently a major influence on William Nash was his father's younger brother Sir Philip Nash, a career railwayman. He took care of William's schooling. During his schooling, somehow Nash was provided with some more than adequate camera equipment.

Nash's mother at the St Bees House, Somerby, built for Mr & Mrs Nash around 1910. The date of this view is *circa* 1916.

Nash's first photographs seem to be of the Ravenglass and Eskdale miniature railway near his St Bees home. These are dated to August 1923 when he was aged 14. He went on to be fascinated by narrow gauge and other minor railways throughout Britain, which leaves us some important images (e.g. of Jersey).

Before long he was working across what is now Cumbria. At Penrith, the old engines of the London and North Western Railway were in their final Indian Summer. Along the coast through Ravenglass to Carnforth, the same could be said of the Furness Railway locomotives. The LMS took time to evolve its visual image and Nash's work shows that transition. He continued to take photographs long enough to see new LMS standard designs like the 'Crabs' and the 'Royal Scots' arrive. Meanwhile his travels enabled fascinating subjects like the change to electric traction on London's Metropolitan Railway, the activities of the three railway companies at Cheltenham, the *Oh! Mr Porter* views of Basingstoke station all to be recorded.

Above : Another Moss postcard, this shows the School House and Chapel, St Bees Grammar School.   *Kate Robinson Collection*

Right: From the many images the one chosen to show the breadth of view in his railway photography is at London's Baker Street station of the then Metropolitan Railway. Already electrified since 1904, it was then in the throes of changing over its first two designs of electric locomotive to a third type which was to be closely associated with the line between 1922 and the early 1960s. Nash photographed all three designs and the Metropolitan's 'K' class 4-4-4T delivered in 1920/21. In the accompanying image is Metropolitan No. 13. This was one of the second design, the 1907 British Thomson-Houston engines. Working out when the picture was taken is a challenge! We are going to say 1923. This is despite some published sources indicating that the engines of this batch were all withdrawn for rebuilding in 1921-22. It is evident from these sources that the term rebuilding was an accounting euphemism. From the manner in which Nash managed to picture all three designs, and from all the evidence that suggests his first pictures were taken in 1923, it seems to us very likely that Nash saw the Metropolitan in the brief time all three classes were in operation. He realised the importance of what he saw and acted accordingly with the camera.

Nash's Basingstoke views are explained by the proximity of a family friend's house who was the Rector of Basingstoke. One of Drummond's ex-London & South Western Railway 'T9' class 4-4-0s passes Basingstoke's engine shed with an up passenger train. The locomotive seen here, No. 120, has survived into preservation and is now part of the National Collection.

Images of the Great Western Railway at Radley link to his schooldays at Radley College which he left prematurely at Easter 1926. A GWR outside-framed 4-4-0 is one of these Radley images. Radley is a station some six miles south of Oxford. The engine is likely to be from the 'Bulldog' class and the train which is unidentified is largely made up of clerestorey coaches. Research has indicated that Radley schoolboys had access to a darkroom.

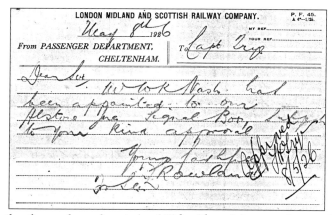

Nash left school apparently after prolonged periods of ill health and it seems he was keen to start work and not continue to study. Only a few weeks after he left school, the General Strike commenced. His mother was at the time living in Cheltenham which led to a substantial block of Cheltenham railway pictures and to Nash being accepted as a volunteer on the LMS there during the strike.

A surviving piece of ephemera is this memo (*above*) appointing Nash 'subject to your kind approval' to work in Alstone Junction signal box. Of itself this memo does not mention the strike and for a moment one might have thought of Alston in Cumbria not Cheltenham. That was LNER not LMS territory and 8th May is several days into the General Strike of 4th-12th May, 1926.

Examining the 1914 Railway Clearing House junction diagrams and the LMS Sectional Appendix found Alstone Junction signal box on the main line between Cheltenham High Street and Lansdown where a 13 chain branch diverged to Alstone Coal Wharf.

That this first appointment was prompted by the strike is followed through by a copy of a rare document (*opposite*). This is the letter that the LMS sent out to volunteers thanking them for their services. The accompanying medal is illustrated on page 103.

Sometime after the General Strike Nash embarked on a career with the LMS which, as promotion came, took him to different locations on the LMS system.

EUSTON STATION.

19th May, 1926.

Dear Sir,

When the Trades Union Council announced their intention to call a General Strike of workers in all Industries, with the object of compelling compliance with the demands of the Miners, the whole Nation, for a moment, was staggered. So soon, however, as the first shock passed, the Government and people set themselves to combat this grave menace, which was recognised by them as a deadly blow aimed at democratic constitutional Government.

With characteristic British courage, Government and people sought new ways and means of carrying on the business of the Country. Volunteers responded to the call for service in overwhelming numbers; the utmost use was made of crippled facilities; the people entered upon their novel tasks with great cheerfulness and surprising adaptability; everywhere there was displayed a ready helpfulness which will outlive many other memories of the struggle; and once again the British race showed that they will not surrender their dearly bought freedom at the dictation of any section of the Community.

The display of these great qualities by you and the many other volunteers who offered their services to the Company enabled the Railway Industry to continue its services to the people, and so make its invaluable contribution to the complete defeat of the scheme to hold up the life of the Community.

I cannot say how much my colleagues on the Board and I, as well as the Company's Officers, value the great help you gave us in meeting this great emergency. We feel that the grave attack on the Community, and the complete defeat, constitute a landmark in the constitutional history of the Country, to which succeeding generations will look back with profound thankfulness. Will you accept our most hearty thanks? The fact that you have so definitely helped to make that bright page in our National history will, I know, be to you a quite sufficient recognition of your valuable services, but I shall, in a short time, ask you to be so good as to accept, as a souvenir, a commemorative medal which we are having struck to mark the occasion.

Yours faithfully,

Guy Granet

W. H. Nash, Esq.
"Rylstone",
Montpelier Parade,
Cheltenham.

Chairman.

Alstone Junction signal box never features in the pictures but it is unlikely to be far from this image. The location was favoured by Nash although other locations in the area included the Honeybourne line and Charlton Kings. Accepting that this picture is somewhere in the 1924-26 period, the rebuilt '2P' engine from the '483' class can be noted as remaining in full Midland Railway livery. Nash noted the train as a Bradford-Paignton express. To stop a moving train was an effective bit of camera work for a teenager in the 1920s.

By the time Nash posed for this picture he was turning 18 and it was January 1927. The exact date when he entered the LMS permanent payroll is not known but it was sometime hereabouts between the General Strike and the item of LMS ephemera from the summer of 1927. The General Strike medal *(above)* carries the inscription *LARGITAS MUNERIS SALUS REIPUBLICAE*, a modern translation of which would be 'generosity of service for the safety of the state'. In the letter sent in January 1927, which accompanied the medal, Mr Stamp, the President of Executive, said, 'I regret that I have not been able to forward the medal earlier, but I hope you will agree that the excellence of the design justifies the time spent in its preparation and execution'.

TELEGRAMS: "TRAINS, CREWE STATION."
TELEPHONE: CREWE, 206.

LONDON MIDLAND AND SCOTTISH RAILWAY COMPANY.

C. R. BYROM,
CHIEF GENERAL SUPERINTENDENT,
DERBY.

S. H. FISHER,
OPERATING ASSISTANT.

CHIEF GENERAL SUPERINTENDENT'S DEPARTMENT.

TRAINS OFFICE.

CREWE.

MY REFERENCE.   YOUR REFERENCE

CP/J.   29th. August 1927.

Dear Sir,

Working Time Book Section 1.

I have received your letter of August 24th and enclosure.

Will you please convey to Clerk Nash my appreciation of the interest and trouble he has taken in going through the proof of the Working Book, and the points he has raised are receiving consideration.

I will bear in mind the question raised at the end of your letter.

Yours faithfully,

Mr. Sykes,
WINDERMERE.

N.B.—PLEASE ADDRESS LETTERS TO "TRAINS OFFICE, CREWE."

This memo of 29th August, 1927 reveals that he was now Clerk Nash, apparently based at Windermere and quite capable of thinking for himself. From this promise it evidently became clear that Nash should be set on a management track. Chapter Two contains a selection of pictures known to have been taken at Carnforth when Nash was working there after his time at Windermere. He was at Carnforth between December 1928 and 1932.

In June 1932 Nash was moved to Crewe where he took many pictures including the diminishing former North Staffordshire Railway stock. This picture shows a Euston-Workington train at Crewe double-headed by two former LNWR engines. They are two 'Claughtons', LMS 5915 *Rupert Guinness* and 5970 *Patience*. William's Crewe address was Claughton Avenue! Sir Gilbert Claughton was the chairman of the London and North Western Railway between 1911-21.

A significant number of images in Central Wales and the Swansea area are also explained by a career move. This impressive shot of Swansea Victoria must date from soon after the advent of these Fowler 2-6-4T. Engine No. 2390 and what is thought to be No. 2403 are about to leave with the 10.15 am over the Central Wales route to Shrewsbury. 2390 went into traffic in June 1933, No. 2403 in September 1933 and these are late railway pictures by Nash who moved there in June 1933.

A chance decision of Nash's to photograph a group of LMS posters and chalk notices confirms that Nash was taking railway pictures in South Wales in July 1933. Nash's position was that of district runner, something like the traffic management trainee of the British Railways period.

Left: A formal portrait of William Nash.

Right: William Nash is seen relaxing at home in Watford *c.*1946 with his friend Wallace M. Snow, who worked for the New York Central System. The New York Central's most prestigious train was the 'Twentieth Century Ltd' which connected New York with Chicago. The motive power used on this service from the 1920s until the 1950s was the celebrated streamlined 'Hudson' class 4-6-4.

Nash evidently was ascending the managerial tree - and he got married. These two factors may help explain what is otherwise a mystery. Somewhere about 1935 he stopped taking railway pictures although other subjects like family holidays continued to be recorded. During World War II he was assistant district controller at Rugby - an important role. Timetable graphs that he prepared for the West Coast Main Line in that period still survive. After the war he went to work at LMS headquarters in London soon to become part of British Railways, London Midland Region.

Nash's railway photography may have lapsed but his interest in what was now his job did not. Amongst items still treasured in the family are his first editions of two significant volumes about Cumbrian railway history that appeared shortly after World War II.

Jack Simmons became a renowned scholar of transport history at Leicester University. One of his earlier works was No. 4 in the Oakwood Library of Railway History, a key contribution to the limited literature of the Maryport and Carlisle Railway. Sadly it seems Nash never photographed that line but he did buy this 1947 book in its hardback edition. The year before W. McGowan Gradon had a key study of the *Furness Railway: Its Rise & Development* in print. Nash bought that too. Nash involved himself in extra-curricular activities like the Worker's Education Association and in learning and using Esperanto. He wrote to railwaymen in Sweden and Hungary using the latter.

All was to be tragically cut short by his death in the Harrow Railway Disaster of 8th October, 1952.

That day he was commuting into London on the 7.31 am from Tring. Behind it was the up Perth sleeper whose driver seemingly managed to ignore three signals in patchy fog and at high speed ran into the local as it left Harrow station. Before anything could be done, the 8 am express out of Euston ploughed into the debris. The disaster claimed 112 lives. Nash was one of the unlucky ones, whilst fellow railway photographer H.C. Casserley, who was another 7.31 am regular, was unable to travel that day because of illness.

Letters of condolence signed and written by key management figures (*see following pages*) in the London Midland structure testify to the regard in which Nash the railway manager was held and the sense of shock and loss felt by his colleagues. Sydney Gould's position was 'Assistant Operating Superintendent LMR (Passenger Services)' in Mr Hearn's office.

Letter 1 (left):

EROS1593

BRITISH RAILWAYS
THE RAILWAY EXECUTIVE
LONDON MIDLAND REGION

S. G. HEARN
Operating Superintendent
S. A. FITCH
Assistant Operating Superintendent
Telephone
EUSTON 1234, EXT
Telegrams
"OPERATING, EUSTON, LONDON"

YOUR REFERENCE

OUR REFERENCE

OPERATING SUPERINTENDENT,
EUSTON HOUSE,
EUSTON STATION,
LONDON, N.W.1

10th October 52

Dear Mrs Nash,

There seem to be no words to express my feelings of sorrow at the sudden loss of your Husband who I knew and liked for many years, and whose unfailing help and support whilst he has been closely associated with me in the last year, I have valued highly.

In offering my deepest sympathy,
I remain,
Yours very sincerely,
Sydney H. Gould

Letter 2 (right):

BRITISH RAILWAYS
THE RAILWAY EXECUTIVE
LONDON MIDLAND REGION

EROS1637

S. G. HEARN
Operating Superintendent
S. A. FITCH
Assistant Operating Superintendent
Telephone
EUSTON 1234, EXT
Telegrams
"OPERATING, EUSTON, LONDON"

YOUR REFERENCE
397.

OUR REFERENCE
OS/10.

OPERATING SUPERINTENDENT,
EUSTON HOUSE,
EUSTON STATION,
LONDON, N.W.1

10th October, 1952.

PERSONAL.

Mrs. W.K. Nash,
89, Ridge Lane,
WATFORD,
Herts.

My dear Mrs. Nash,

It has now been officially confirmed, and you will have been advised, that your husband was a victim of the tragic accident at Harrow & Wealdstone Station on 8th October. I wish to convey to you and your family my deepest sympathy with you all in your bereavement and irreparable loss.

Your husband worked very closely with me in regard to certain matters and I formed the highest opinion of his ability and character. I feel sure many of his colleagues would wish to be associated with this tribute to his memory.

You will shortly be approached about your future welfare, but at the moment I feel I must say how much we all feel for you in this great tragedy, which I know you will bear with fortitude and courage.

Yours sincerely,
S. G. Hearn

British Railways letter

BRITISH RAILWAYS
THE RAILWAY EXECUTIVE
LONDON MIDLAND REGION

ER051637

S. G. HEARN
Operating Superintendent
B. A. FITCH
Assistant Operating Superintendent
Telephone
EUSTON 1234, EXT 397.
Telegrams
"OPERATING, EUSTON, LONDON"

YOUR REFERENCE

OUR REFERENCE
OS/10.

OPERATING SUPERINTENDENT,
EUSTON HOUSE,
EUSTON STATION,
LONDON, N.W.1

16th October, 1952.

Mrs. W.K. Nash,
89, Ridge Lane,
WATFORD,
HERTS.

Dear Mrs. Nash,

When the Royal train arrived at Euston on Tuesday morning the Queen's Equerry enquired about your husband and asked for details to be sent to Buckingham Palace. I have this morning received a letter from Sir Michael Adeane saying :-

"Her Majesty is very sorry indeed to hear about Mr. William Kenneth Nash, who lost his life in the accident at Harrow and Wealdstone and who was a member of your staff and had been concerned with arrangements for the Royal train.

The Queen would be grateful if you would convey her sincere sympathy to his family."

I transmit this message to you with my own great sorrow, because, as I told you in my letter the other day, I feel his loss as a personal one.

Yours sincerely,

S. G. Hearn

Staff Travel card

Staff Travel   01.04.00 to 30.06.01   1st

Surname   Forename
NASH   MARJORY
WIDOW(ER)   A 683810
Endorsements (see over) [NIL]
DATES MUST NOT BE ALTERED   A683810

Issuing Location PENSIONS DARLINGTON

Life went on, the railway was a great community and the unified British Railways did (maybe not always perfectly) look after its own. Travel concessions for the staff and their dependents were until recent years far more generous than they are in the privatised environment of the 21st century. Railways were to be a favoured form of transport for Nash's three daughters until they achieved their majority aged 21. And many years after that, how fortunate it was that the youngest daughter Kate, by now an able photographer herself, decided that her father's photos should be put before a wider audience.

Bibliography

The literature about railway photography is vast. Details of some books are given that will either describe other railway photographers active before World War II or provide more information about the Cumbrian railway scene and the trains that Nash photographed.

A Compendium of LNWR Locomotives: Willie B. Yeadon, Challenger Publications, 1995.
British Railways Past and Present No. 1 Cumbria: John Broughton and Nigel Harris, Silver Link Publishing, 1985.
Eric Treacy: John Peart-Binns, Ian Allan, 1980.
Famous Railway Photographers: H.C. Casserley: H.C. Casserley, David and Charles, 1972.
Famous Railway Photographers: P. Ransome-Wallis: P. Ransome-Wallis, David and Charles, 1973.
Furness Railway: Locomotives and Rolling Stock: R.W. Rush, Oakwood Press, 1973.
My Best Railway Photographs: a series published by Ian Allan from 1946 featuring the work of O.J. Morris, P. Ransome-Wallis, H.C. Casserley, Maurice W. Earley, Eric Treacy and nine others.
Furness Railway A View From The Past: Howard Quayle, Ian Allan, 2000.
Great Railway Photographs by Eric Treacy: G. Freeman Allen, Peerage Books, 1987.
Railways Between the Wars: H.C. Casserley, David and Charles, 1971.
Ratty's 100: Douglas Ferreira, Ravenglass and Eskdale Railway, 1976.
Spell of Steam: Eric Treacy, Ian Allan 1973.
The Furness Railway 1843-1923: R.W. Rush, Oakwood Press, 1973.
The Ravenglass and Eskdale Railway: W.J.K. Davies, David and Charles, 1981.
The Ravenglass and Eskdale Railway A Journey Through Historic Postcards: David Jenner, Adrian Smith, Peter Van Zeller, Ravenglass and Eskdale Railway, 1991.
Vintage Album 1850-1925: J.E. Kite, Roundhouse Books, 1966.